SpeedLearning

Selected Works
of
W. A. Mozart

The Buckley Notation System

Created by
William F. Buckley, Jr.

Compiled and edited by Judith Norell

Editorial supervision: Edward Capano, Edward Shanaphy
Project coordinator: Julia Peña

Table of Contents

How to Increase Your Learning Speed

The Buckley Notation System

By William F. Buckley, Jr.

PHOTO BY JAN LUCAS

I began playing (or rather, trying to play) the piano at age seven, which was fifty-five years ago. My teacher, to whom at age eight I proposed, and whom, at age eighty, I love as much as ever, was something of a perfectionist. It is my only criticism of her that she did not teach sight-reading as a distinct skill. She would think nothing of spending nine months on the first movement of the Appassionata Sonata, to get everything *exactly* right: which means that at the end of nine months, you have got exactly right, subject to the limitations of your technique, the first movement of one Beethoven sonata — leaving behind one hundred sonatas you might have familiarized yourself with.

I don't have the figures, but I wouldn't be surprised if ninety per cent of the people who study the piano as children never touch it as adults, and it has always haunted me why this should be so. Every two or three years I have revved up and tackled something (the harpsichord is now my chosen instrument) and I even performed a concerto in the fall of 1989, but damned if it didn't take me *fourteen months* to learn the thing. These, however, may prove to have been the most profitable fourteen months of practice I ever undertook; because I made a discovery. No, I made two discoveries. Actually, two and one half discoveries.

Someone had told me, years and years ago, that it always helps, if you want to familiarize yourself with a piece as fast as possible, to write down every single item of fingering. No matter *how obvious it is.* If you see "2" on the C, "3" on the D, and "5" on the F, pick up a pencil and write "4" over the E, no matter how plain it is that that is the finger intended.

I did this to my concerto. But I went one step further. Every time my finger would cross, I would give myself a warning — through the simple device of circling the finger that hits that note just before the fingers cross. So that I might see "1" on the C, "2" on the D, " 3 " (circled) on the E; then I would know ahead of time that I was about to use the "1" again, on the F, or whatever. As I picked up the pace, it helped me hugely to have some advance notice that I was about to cross my fingers.

And then there is the problem of black keys. I know, I know, there are people out there who have merely to spot the two sharps on the clef, know that they are playing in D major, and obviously all F's and C's are sharped — and if you get an accidental, why, it is marked an accidental. And — obviously — if it is accidental at the beginning of a measure, so is it elsewhere in that same measure; and the blasé notation people, over the centuries, have not bothered to repeat the accidental mark (why should they? They already told you, you lazy jerk) any more than it would occur to them to remind you that every C and every F are black keys.

Well, not for me; no longer; never. On my Bach F Minor Concerto I red-inked *every single black key note.* Yup. At no point, in that concerto, would I not know, ahead of time, that I was headed for a black key. And it made no difference to me whatever that I should have known it was a black key intuitively, or intellectually. The fact of the matter is: I was forwarding an objective, which is to shorten the time it takes to learn to play a piece.

Now I say: Try it. Try using the Buckley Notation System, and see if you don't learn pieces in half the time it usually takes. By the way, the fingering has been done by one of my teachers, the great virtuoso Judith Norell. I will *not* answer any correspondence reproaching me for using the third finger instead of the fourth on any particular note, and I will protect Judith by not giving out her address.

If you like the idea, please write to us and let us know. With sufficient encouragement we will happily provide more composer collections with this hospitable notation. A few years of this and we'll all be reporting to Ft. Worth for the Van Cliburn contest.

■

How to Practice Mozart

My Method

By Judith Norell

Judith Norell

I studied piano and harpischord, for over 15 years, and was never taught how to practice. It took lots of wasted time, and many painful experiments to realize that *playing* and *practicing* are different. It was only in 1985, when I had a limited time to learn the complete harpischord works of Bach for his tricentennial anniversary, that I took the trouble to devise a system for myself. This system works on any baroque, classical or romantic composer.

Learning music can be divided into two elements: the technical and the musical. Each must be approached separately, and then mixed – some technical work followed by some musical work, until the piece is completely mastered.

Technical Elements

1. Read through the piece as best as you can, with both hands, to give yourself an idea of how difficult it is.

2. At a slow tempo, play *each hand separately,* paying attention to the fingerings. Try not to stop, but if you do, note with an asterisk or other mark, where you stopped, and another asterisk where you think the difficult section ends.

3. Go back to the difficult spots which you have marked. In each section, choose a point a few notes before the difficulty starts, and slowly and carefully play from that point to a few notes beyond the end of that section. Repeat this several times, until you can play it smoothly without stopping.

4. Do not rush to play faster – you will be able to, particularly if you restrain yourself now.

5. Slowly play both hands together, again marking where you have difficulty. Practice those sections separately.

6. Make a point at every other practice session to start at the second half of the piece, or at the double bar line.

Musical Elements

The human voice naturally gives a musical shape to the tunes it sings, but the keyboard, whether piano, organ or harpischord, can do anything the player wants it to, regardless of whether it is integral to the musical line or not, therefore it is very important to approach music as a singer would. In Mozart, the right hand usually plays the melody, although occasionally the left hand has lines or fragments of melody as well. The best way to decide how a piece should be played is to sing it, and then try to translate it to the keyboard.

1. Take a melody in the right-hand of the piece you are playing, and try to sing it out loud. (Singing silently or humming doesn't help.) Mozart's dynamic markings of *forte* and *piano* are minimal, and it is important to shape the music yourself. Listen to where you have to take a breath, to where your voice gets louder or softer, to where you sing staccato or legato. Think of it as a game, and have fun doing it. You can even make up words to the melodies. Sing to yourself *out loud* when you go for a walk, or in the bathtub or shower, and *listen* to what you are doing with your voice. Try to play the way you sing. If you forget what you have sung, mark the music to remember. Do the same for the left hand whenever it seems to have a fragment of melody.

2. Put both hands together, and make sure that their dynamic levels are balanced; when the left hand accompanies, it should be softer than the right, but when the left hand has the melody, it must be brought out.

3. Check on yourself to see whether the way you want the music to sound is the way it is coming out through your fingers, and whether you like it like that. If you do, fine. If you don't, sing it again before changing it.

Technical and Musical Polishing

1. From the slow, careful tempo you have been practicing speed up a notch, but don't get too fast. If you have been listening to yourself, you will know at what tempo you eventually want to play the piece, but

always increase your tempo in small increments, and keep listening.

2. If you can play at the increased speed but there are still a few technical difficulties, single out those passages, particularly where there are many sixteenth notes, and play them slower using different rhythms to trick your fingers into negotiating the notes well. E.g. if you have a passage with lots of ♪♪♪♪ s, practice it as ♪♪♪♪ and as ♪♪♪♪ until you can play it smoothly both ways.

Above all, try to value practicing as a pleasure in and of itself. It is fun to listen to the beautiful tones that come out of your instrument, to feel your finger muscles stroking the keys, and to become more competent in interpreting the music of Mozart.

Ornaments

Mozart's ornaments can be confusing. Should they be played on or before the beat, slow or fast, where should they be placed in a moving passage, etc? Should a passage be played differently if he wrote as ornament the first time, and then wrote out notes the second time (e.g. sonata in A minor K 310, m. 2 appoggiatura vs. m. 10, eighth notes)? There are no absolute answers but the following are some suggestions culled from many years of experience:

1. The *Appoggiatura* – was often used when a dissonance occurred between the melody and the accompanying left hand harmony, and whether short or fast, was always written with a slash:

2. The *Turn* – sometimes fully written out (e.g. Rondo in F Major, K 494; see mm. 38, 39) but is often expressed by the symbol ∞. It sometimes begins *on* the note and sometimes on the note *above*. If may have to be fitted in between moving notes, but is sometimes used in freer passages:

3. The *Trill* – In Mozart's time trills could begin on the note itself or on the note above the written note; they could be short or end abruptly; with or without an inverted mordent; they could gradually increase in speed, as if improvised. Mozart rarely noted which he wanted and it is left to the player to choose. *Trill fingerings* have been given according to which note it was felt the trill should begin on; only the first few fingerings have been noted, whether the trill is short or extended. If a trill fingering reads 323212, the 12 usually refers to the inverted mordent to appear at the end of the trill, giving it a more gradual and graceful end. Time and practice will allow the player to decide what is appropriate for his or her own technical level and musical taste. Mozart improvised, so should we!

■

Three Minuets

RONDO
in D Major

13

16

SONATA
in C Major

19

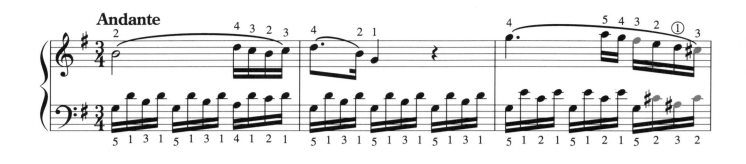

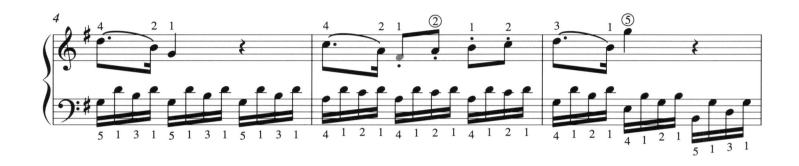

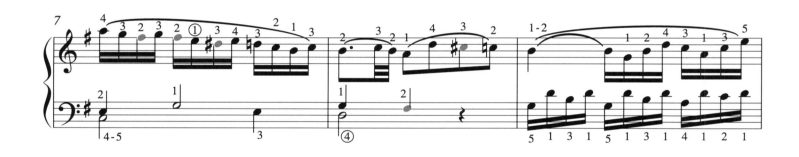

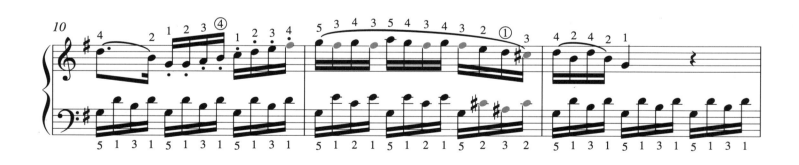

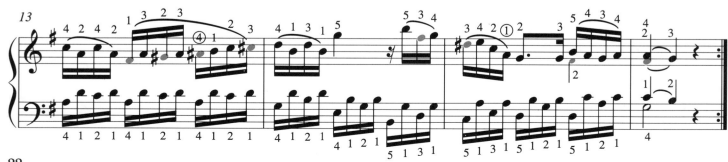

Allegretto

26

27

RONDO
in F Major

K 494

30

31

33

Fantasy
in D minor

K 397

36

Tempo I

39

March
in C Major

41

Sonata
in A Major (Turkish March)

VAR. II

VAR. III

VAR. IV

VAR. V

Adagio (♪ = 72)

VAR. VI

Allegro (♩ = 120)

50

Trio

Alla Turca

Allegretto (♩ = 132)

55

56

Twelve Variations on "Ah, vous dirai-je, Maman"

K 265

THEMA

VAR. II

VAR. III

VAR. IV

VAR. V

VAR. VI

VAR. VII

VAR. VIII

VAR. IX

VAR. X

VAR. XI

Adagio (♩ = 44)

RONDO
in A minor

K 511

73

SONATA
in A minor

K 310

Allegro maestoso (♩ = 108)

ca . . . . . . lan . . . . . . do

Andante cantabile con espressione (♩ = 58)

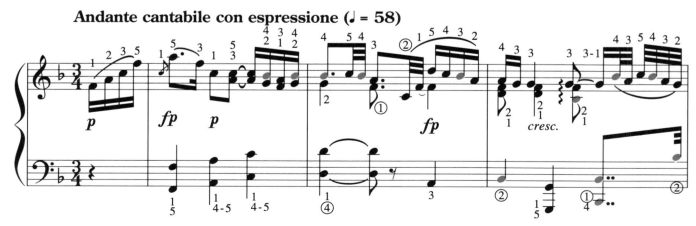

Presto (♩ = 152)

1000 KEYBOARD IDEAS

★ **For Musicians Of All Levels!**

★ **Sound Like A Pro!**

★ **Pop, Jazz and Classical!**

This thoroughly revised and improved version of "Keyboard Tricks Of The Trade," the most popular guide ever to better keyboard playing, has even MORE of the tips and tricks used by professionals to create their great sounds! There are sections on harmony, voicings, style, pop, rock and jazz playing, technique, sight-reading, memorizing, practice tips and more. Over 330 pages in all!

Whether you want advice on jazz runs or chords, country fills, bass lines and stride patterns ... the ins and outs of novelty piano ... beautiful harmonic colors and syncopated rhythms ... organ effects ... improvising ... or a guide on how to get your fingers to move more easily across the keys ... you'll find it all here under one cover!

A Musical Encyclopedia Of Style!

Each section contains dozens of articles on the topics you want ... so you can browse to your heart's content, or choose just the information you are looking for! 1,000 Keyboard Ideas is a virtual encyclopedia of information on playing keyboards for more enjoyment and satisfaction! You'll want to keep it close to your instrument month after month!

Your Guarantee

Try 1000 Keyboard Ideas for a full 30 days. If you don't agree it is the best guide ever to professional-sounding keyboard playing, simply return it for a full refund. No questions asked! It's our no-nonsense guarantee of your satisfaction. So order your copy TODAY!

HOW TO ORDER

To order, write down your name and address (including zip code), and the number of copies of 1000 Keyboard Ideas you want. For each book ordered, enclose check or money order for $24.95 payable to Songbooks Unlimited. Add $3.25 postage and handling. (NJ and IA residents please add sales tax.) Include the product number of the book, #900258. Or, CHARGE IT to your MasterCard or Visa. Include your account number and expiration date. Mail to: SONGBOOKS UNLIMITED, Dept. 097519, P.O. Box 11061, Des Moines, IA 50336-1061. We will ship promptly with full 30-day money-back guarantee.

For Fastest Service Call Toll Free 1-800-527-6300, 24 Hours A Day, 7 Days A Week!

A Wonderful Collection For Every Pianist!

20 Piano's Greatest Hits

Here are some of the most beautiful, most requested and most cherished pieces for piano in a collection that will earn a very special place on your music shelf. It's as if someone selected just the good parts from the piano repertoire, the most wonderful melodies and haunting themes, the pieces that are the most fun and the most satisfying to play ... and put them all together in one convenient place!

You'll find the famous Tango by Albeniz ... Beethoven's plaintive "Für Elise" ... the intoxicating colors of Debussy's "Clair de Lune" ... Scott Joplin's lilting "Solace" (the Mexican serenade from the movie "The Sting") ... the soaring theme from Rachmaninoff's Second Piano Concerto ... Erik Satie's simple and touching "Gymnopedie No. 1" ... and so much more. There are 20 immortal piano hits in all. You'll want to savor each one over and over again!

Your Guarantee

We are sure you will be thrilled with 20 Piano's Greatest Hits. But if you are unsatisfied for any reason at all, simply return it within 30 days for a full refund. No questions asked. You have absolutely nothing to lose, so order your copy TODAY!

Tango *Isaac Albeniz* • **Prelude** *Bach/Siloti* • **Adagio From "Moonlight Sonata"** *Ludwig van Beethoven* • **Für Elise** *Ludwig van Beethoven* • **Prelude In E minor** *Frederic Chopin* • **Clair de Lune** *Claude Debussy* • **Poeme** *Zdenko Fibich* • **Music For The Royal Fireworks** *George Frideric Handel* • **Solace** *Scott Joplin* • **To A Wild Rose** *Edward MacDowell* • **Oriental** *J. Ruiz Manzanares* • **Elegie** *Jules Massenet* • **Spring Song** *Felix Mendelssohn* • **Rondo alla Turca** *Wolfgang Amadeus Mozart* • **Odeon** *Ernesto Nazareth* • **Canon** *Johann Pachelbel* • **Theme From Piano Concerto No. 2** *Sergei Rachmaninoff* • **Gymnopedie No. 1** *Erik Satie* • **Traümerei** *Robert Schumann* • **Larghetto** *Igor Stravinsky* •

Because you bought this book ...
Here's a
Money-Saving Offer

Sheet Music Magazine *brings you the songs you love to play*

We print lots of songs, *right in our magazine,* that are the most popular, best-loved songs ever written. And we don't just print the words. You get all the music too, with full sheet music arrangements ... PLUS ... lots of great tips and lessons from the pros to get you playing your best. In fact, there's an entire **music workshop** section in each issue which is used by thousands of music teachers and their students nationwide.

Above all, **Sheet Music Magazine** is a music magazine for amateur at-home musicians who just like to relax and have fun with their music. When your first issue arrives in the mail, we guarantee you'll drop everything and head to your piano or guitar, or maybe you'll just start singing right there by the mailbox. You get at least a dozen songs with each and every issue. And what great songs they are. The exciting songs of today, the golden hits of yesteryear. The love songs. The fun songs. The somebody done somebody wrong songs. It's the perfect answer for a good old fashioned sing-along party too.

Now Save 10%!

Let us send you your first jumbo, jam-packed issue with no obligation whatsoever. If you decide to cancel we'll send you your money back, and you may keep the special first issue as our gift. And that will end the matter. That's our way of saying thanks for giving us a try. If you do keep your subscription — or if you already subscribe and want to renew — we'll take 10% off our regular price of $15.97 as a special gift for purchasing this book! You pay just $14.37.

So order TODAY. You have absolutely nothing to lose ... *and lots of good music in store!*

Sheet Music Magazine ... the world's most popular music magazine.

Here are 20 Great Songs included in your first issue of Sheet Music Magazine ...

Evergreen • Together • As Time Goes By • A Time For Love • Somewhere My Love • After The Lovin' • Morning Has Broken • Three Little Words • It Had To Be You • The Sound of Silence • Rose Garden • Chattanooga Choo Choo • Crying • Misty • Born To Lose • From A Distance • Tennessee Waltz • It All Depends On You • I've Got A Crush On You

This offer is our way of introducing this exciting song magazine to people who love to play music.

Sheet Music Magazine

P.O. Box 58629, Boulder, CO 80322-8629

YES, SEND MY Introductory Issue and enter my subscription (or Renewal) to Sheet Music Magazine as a 10% savings as checked below. I understand that I may cancel after receiving the free issue and receive a 100% refund of my payment — no questions asked!

I enclose full payment of $_____
(Make check payable to Sheet Music Magazine)
Charge to: ☐ MasterCard   ☐ Visa

Account No._____ Exp. Date_____

(√) check one
☐ Standard Piano (Guitar)
☐ Easy Play
☐ This is a New Subscription

(√) check one
☐ One Year (6 issues) $14.37
☐ Two Years (12 issues) $26.00
☐ This is a Renewal

Name _____
Address _____
City _____ State _____ Zip _____

Canadian residents please add $2.00 per year extra for postage.

5R121